Alien Crop

For Des
and for my father

Il n'y a pas de morts – *there are no dead.*
Maurice de Maeterlinck – L'Oiseau bleu IV ii

Alien Crop

Janet Paisley

Chapman Publishing
2004

Chapman Publishing
4 Broughton Place
Edinburgh EH1 3RX
Scotland

First published 1996
Reprinted 2004

This book was first published with the assistance of
the Deric Bolton Trust and the Scottish Arts Council

A catalogue record for this volume is
available from the British Library
ISBN 1-903700-09-4
Chapman New Writing: Wild Women Series
Editor Joy Hendry
ISSN 0953-5306

© Janet Paisley 2004
Janet Paisley is hereby identified as the author of
this work in accordance with Section 77 of the
Copyright, Design and Patents Act 1988

All rights are strictly reserved
Requests to reproduce the text in whole or in part
should be addressed to the publisher

Cover by Fred Crayk

Some poems have appeared in the following magazines: *Chapman, Lines Review, Spectrum, Northlights, Northwords, Squibs, Scottish Child, New Voices, Glasgow Herald, Teaching English, Interarts, Poetry North, Gown, Empathy, Scot Free, The Pometry Diary, Original Prints, Scottish International Poetry Competition Anthology, Poetry Society Competition Anthology, Shelter Anthology, Write round the Circle, Revolving Showcase, Best of Poetry Now, Images, Pegasus in Flight, Biting through Skins, Modern Scottish Women Poets, Ars Poetica, Scottish Poetry Library Postcards;* and broadcast on BBC educational radio, Radio Scotland, Radio Clyde, KLT and ITV's *In Verse*; on stage in *Saturday Night & Sunday Mourning, The Killing of Women, Stick* and *Cartographies of Desire.*

Printed by Colourbooks, Unit 105, Baldoyle Industrial Estate,
Baldoyle, Dublin 13, Eire

Contents

Things I Do Not Know / *7*
Things You Do Not Know / *7*
Trust / *8*
North Glasgow College / *8*
Sinking the Ship / *9*
Conjugate / *9*
Seasoning the Solstice / *10*
Seriously Though / *11*
Spellbinding / *12*
Scattered Seed / *13*
Incalculable Infidelities / *14*
Bittersweet / *15*
Equinox / *16*
Cold Turkey / *17*
Haiku / *18*
Crow / *19*
Beyond Recall / *20*
Seeking Spring / *21*
Alien Crop / *22*
Don't Say You Love Me, Daddy / *23*
Old Man's Chair / *24*
Togetherness / *24*
Battered / *25*
The Rainmaker / *26*
Easy Street / *27*
The List / *28*
The Trek / *30*
Words for my Daughter / *31*
Borrowed from the Mother / *32*
Witchcraft / *34*
Gothic? / *34*
Woman in Rags / *35*
Storm Warning / *36*
The Ashtray / *37*
Selling It / *38*
Squaring the Circle / *39*
The Gathering / *41*

While Pruning / *42*
Wild Cherry / *43*
Bonfire / *44*
Praise the Lord / *45*
Ride with the Hunters / *47*
Critical Distance / *48*
The Caul / *49*
Prematurely Beached / *50*
Ceremony of Sorrow / *51*
The Village / *52*
Matthew / *53*
The Last Bell / *54*
Divisions / *55*
Momentary Fox / *56*
Tidal Seal / *57*
Water of Lethe / *58*
Absolutely / *59*
Excuses of a Romantic / *60*
Not Coming Home / *61*
Homeless / *62*
Three Ravens / *63*
Stock and Barrel / *64*
Old Horse / *65*
Frog / *66*
Biting Through Skins / *67*
Poem with No Name / *68*

Biographical Note / *71*

Things I Do Not Know

the taste of your skin
the pulse of your heart
the touch of your breath
the moment of your waking
the shape of your sleep

Things You Do Not Know

my mind open to engage you
my body open to absorb you
my soul open to resolve you
my hand open to let you go

Trust

There can be no keeping
for rainbows will not be kept
though startled eyes still print
the spectrum on closed lids.
Before light comes, dark comes,
and circles repeat. Cyclic,
as rain to river to sea,
we come together,
are bound to come together;
the tide swells and subsides.
Reaching for each other
in the dark, we rise to light
— you move me to belief
in what has always been
and somewhere in the desert
a flower unfolds, unseen.

North Glasgow College

Coming out into cold night
I need to cross the distance
to where you are; a long leap
over desperate oceans,

taken on trust. Your touch
steadies me, our mouths meet
giving blood heat assurance
as your arms gather me in.

That's where belief is; you
being there, certain as breath,
stoking slow fires against frost
to wait the quickening spring.

Sinking the Ship

I am awash with you, floundering
as flood breaches hull and stern.
Fingering my spine, you slide
deep inside me, spill
your whole salt self into my hold
and surging now, surround, enclose.
With a clasp more terrible than earth
you draw me down. This shifting tomb
is fathomless, a slow, complete caress
that year by year will strip me to the bone
yet my last breath, sinking, drowning,
still cries 'Yes' – and silenced
to the shaken stillness of accord,
love. Love is too small a word.

Conjugate

Tensely
premenstrual and
looping the full moon
I am seriously
deranged yet
curiously
in possession of
all my faculties

consumed by
feeling for you
biology stands on its head.
What is instead
consummate
in this desire is
I'm seriously
dispossessed.

Seasoning the Solstice

I would give you winter
hot in skin scorched fragments,
hard as frost, deep as ice,
the bite burned into flesh,
a scalding truth. Armed
with fire we could consume
the frozen face of fear.

I would give you a spring
spun in sugar, like leaves
burst in dreams, sweet on tongues
of desire, streams sparkling
as the blood running
free in life's vein. My love,
we could turn the earth green.

I would give you summer
calm as warmth, smooth as love
in the long slow heat haze
of everyday. Sand-grained
we'd make time shimmer
into glass. Tomorrows
reflected, we could last.

I would give you autumn
frivolous but turning
towards slow bedding down.
A casting of old coats
to prepare new skin,
cool as deep ringed water
we could make perfect sleep.

Seriously Though

Poets stay young, that's the thing
and if you intend
        to take offence
at every giggle
        or hug, I mean
if you seriously intended to slide
slowly, but with great haste, into
old age,
        well maybe, just maybe
when I rage a little (or a great deal)
or spin round in the rain
        with my wet mouth
wanting
        to be kissed, or kick the air
and let my hair skiff the ground
leaning back on some swing
in a park
        somewhere while trying
to fly higher, ever higher
        towards the sun
knowing all about the risks
of melting wax
        and not caring what a fool
I've been (or might become)
        or if
I need to wake you
        at 3am to make love
(when there's a full moon of course)
outside
        in the long grass, hands grasping
the rough bark of tree skin
        well, maybe
maybe if you're not there,
        you won't,
seriously,
        be missed.

Spellbinding

You carry her
in your pocket
like a stone.
Every now and then,
touching her name
for comfort.
Ideas blossom
in a burst of words
and with it, love
but still that single
syllable returns,
slots into place
on your tongue,
brings familiar taste
to pin you down.
She stops you
spinning into space,
anchors where you feel.
Unrealised fear
of weakening ties
creates your need
to speak the spell
that is her name.
You bind yourself.
Called up again
that solid word
drops in the drift
of conversation.
The stone you cast
to shatter surface,
fragments an image
we've conjured with.

Scattered Seed

So, you woke with my name in your mouth
at 3 am, my time to make love
when the cat steps out on the tiles
and the last poem is put to bed.
And what was it you said woke you, the sound?

So, you woke with my name in your mouth
and did it slip off your tongue
like melted butter from hot bread
spilling in warm streams from moist lips
or was it stuck like grape pips in your teeth?

And did you swallow the flesh of it,
spit out the inedible bits,
turn to the real woman beside you
having had me inside out
to abandon as empty skin. Did you wake

to the level of denying your dreams?

Incalculable Infidelities

I am hard pressed against your wall,
breast bruised, winded. Trumpetless
and torn, I fall away. Now,
limping the long path home, I am sworn
to not return. No more ditches, I'm done
with seeking warmth from grave trenches
where chill ices bone. Don't look for me
in shallow morning coffee cups, don't reach
for any telephone. The end of it
is ringing out – loneliness, you split me
with an incalculable ache of it.
The axe-welt flowers open, blood-free,
tear-free, blossoming with pain. Oh,
and I stood, again and again, absorbing
the blunted stun of such sharp force
as would have had you scream release.
Touch me, hold me, meet me whole
– unspoken words, you couldn't read
any need of mine. Our world spins down
to balance on the pinpoint of your fear;
Jerico. And I of no discernable account,
betrayed by every faithless night.
My love, I'll rewrite history,
keep safe behind your walls
while I remove to bind the gaping wound
you would not fill. I will re-make
a kind of wholeness in the silence,
soundless, leave no music in your soul.

Bittersweet

The Trailblazer cherry blooms
mocking your departure;
clustered aubergine buds split,
cup each small white flower.

Not the first tree keeping tryst;
the Kilmarnock Willow weeps
yellow catkins, has done for weeks

and other flowerings came first.
Primroses braved the frost with flags
blue, white and gold and blush;
new-startled eyes now open wide

as cherry branches rush at sky,
upright, unbending, strive
against the riot of distraction.

Blossom bursts free of hard wood,
pale petals bright, sunstroked
with light and shade; a pretty picture
that will yield to bitter fruit.

How easily you drove away.

Equinox

today should be spring
the weatherman on TV says Aberdeen
is warmer than Rome

where I am living
winter tightens its grip

I lean on the cold shoulder
but fail to draw
a curative of angry heat

illness rampages
past all my lost defences

sorrow seducing sickness
through the hours of day and night
evenly divided

I am in the East
you are in the West

what possible significance can that have

Cold Turkey

Head on the chopping block again,
I should have been named Mary.

Holy Mary

Sick from working through stress
my kidneys decide on bed rest.

Mother of God

The pain turns me over,
sweating, wanting amputation
at the waist.

Pray for us sinners now

The weight in my chest
is not diagnosed.
I told you not to phone, ever.
You haven't phoned.

and at the hour of our death

My mother, who is not Jewish
brings me chicken soup.

Haiku

you were light to me
and everywhere sunsets
leave dark oceans

evening valley
full of mountainous shadow
that cannot be climbed

when words are not flesh
in the skeletal remains
how thin my poems are

Crow

through a white blind
                          cold blue light
outside, a bird
      sends singular notes
                            lightly strung
      sound opals
                  they ball
harmlessly round
                bouncing on grass
                falling
      they do not rise
    to breakthrough
do not shatter
                          glass air

it must be a blackbird
                not a crow
   the crow is in here
where he often is
                          these days
watching
    from the silent piano
claws draped on wood
                      he shuffles
rearranges his gown
                thumbs hooked in
positions
            the tilt of his head
asks the question

Beyond Recall

I am no ghost; put
your hand on my breast,
feel the pulse; time
passes through me; I
pay my dues and choose
to live. Things we keep
in boxes cannot look
up or down, or move.
From dusty corners
they call out, thin threads
of once fat loves in need
of food. I will not be
stored against the drought;
grain for grain I plant
gardens and move on.

This is no echo
of a sound once heard
some wild fool moon. Dark,
the splintering heart
wood cracks to brightness
in the sun. Life is won
in waking from soul-sleep.
I will not be pressed
to serve your dreams; touch
my flesh, I sweat; blood
over-spills a cut
deep to the bone. I don't
whisper in the wind;
I speak with tongues, cry
out, rage, shout at stone.

I hold against you,
feel the heat; this shape
has taste and substance.
No haunting; eyes smile,
and weep, and stare. Press;
the imprint of your hands
scald-mark the skin. You
cannot iron flat
a full, round, wholeness,
pack this memory;
I am real. Our feelings
demonstrate or lie
in dying words. I
will not keep; only shadows
do not walk away.

Seeking Spring

Remembering, I go down
the long winter valley
where under quilted snow
cold silence curls dumbly.

And yes, I know the way
down to the glassy river
whose ranks of guardian reeds
glitter sharply silver.

Again ice cuts my knuckles,
I dig my fingers raw
hoping deep down is water
and somewhere, surely, thaw.

Alien Crop

So the boats come in,
charcoal shadows etched on liquid gold –
she is not always so fine a mistress,
her depths combed smooth with light.
I have waited through nights
of her grey lady, webbed with mist
while she whispered her possession
on the bloodless stone. I have watched
her raking claws rise, a green harlot
shrieking spit, jealously making
her grave bed ready below the heaving sheets.
This dusk is still and holds the cat-purr
of engine and the call of voices,
clear on shore as if an echo sounded near.
You will come, a stranger dying in your eyes,
that man I have never known, tasting of tears,
salt fingerings in your hair,
her blood kisses whitening on your mouth.
I know only your feet at the fireside,
your hungers and your tossing sleep
the wearing of you and the leavings.
It has been a long standing between us,
these dry shore waits but now, on this late tide
I feel the child swell within me.
I will wait your landfall, the wet
song of rope, the scrape of wood, the alien
crop of you, and know a new strangeness
for I, too, am fishing
in the drift of a setting sun.

Don't Say You Love Me, Daddy

Don't say you love me, Daddy,
then it's all right.
I am your loving daughter
At night I hide in the cracked wall
making myself. Becoming so small
you do not see that body under you
does not belong to me.
You teach grown up things
and I don't understand any of it
except mother is crazy and blind.
That's why you are unkind to her.
Sometimes, from my hiding place,
I sing a tiny song.
Thin as thread in a needle
my voice is not strong enough
to stitch me well.
I'm a monster who can't tell.
Words would make you real
then I'd feel and I don't, I don't.
Can't move, make a sound now
but when you're not around
I burst your eyes on my nails,
prise your tongue out of my mouth,
shred your skin, stick
the kitchen knife into your heart.
I make hate then, to live on,
and you can't take that too
when I hide it inside a deep wall.
So just don't say you love me,
Daddy. That's all.

Old Man's Chair

This is the arm chair where he sat;
Old leather, worn, stuffed with hair.
She will burn it now he's gone.

And if we had no memories
that would be that. An old man's chair,
a puff of smoke, a childhood done.

But what will we do with remembering
when it uncurls, and crawls
between us – keep silent still?

Or will we talk, and turn, re-make
the summers that we sat in,
break each other's hearts then heal.

Or has he won?

Togetherness

When all the words are put back in the chest
we'll carry it, two handed, to the garden.
There, we'll bury it and hurry back inside.

There will be no cross to mark the spot,
the grass will grow and cover it. No-one
will ever know what lies hidden there.

We will forget, a few feet from our door
lies every word we ever said. Silence
will sleep between us, undisturbed.

And in some future time, others will come
and, digging to reclaim the wilderness
to make their garden, will strike a store

of words that have been spoken once before.

Battered

The yard shines white
each brick, each blade of grass outlined
the garage sharp, dark planes
an edge, the light –
the fields fluoresce – the moon full, mocks
an O of open mouth
eyes round, surprised –
can this be night?
Darker than all the nights – she jests
her fulsome tricks do not impress
I live with madness she projects –
each month we stare this vigil
each month she stares, amazed
each time I gape, blind in every quarter
blank inside my mind.
How do I find relief –
like this moon-thief I cannot cry
she is dust dry, rock dead
– battered –
as battered and as dead as I
she does not live, simply reflects.
Life would scream and shout
but having none
– so silently –
we stare each other out.

The Rainmaker

We waited a long time for the rains coming.
Dry, our tongues cracked on words
that might have healed the wounded desert.
Rivers, how long since they flowed?

We measured time in hacks.
Fissures that had forgotten how to thirst
deepened and did not know to bleed.
Seeds were powder, grey ash

an ant could make wind enough to stir.
But wind portends, and there was none.
We parted air in hot curtains,
breathed shallow from tormented lungs.

The hawking cry of tempted speech
was not enough to break
the shivering pillars of a tempered sky.
Knee deep in burning sand, we salted

grooves where tears should run.
When the man came, we saw
the empty sockets and his brain on fire.
Skeletal hands pointed where his belly

once had been. The dying child screamed –
a sound that curdled air and moving
kept the currents drift astir.
The temple shattered into jagged shards,

and onto drying vision drove the clouds.
White puffs, then banking grey they wheeled,
a blackened army spitting steel.
We turned our faces to the spikes,

felt leathered skins soak soft, and down
our ravined throats the water coursed.
Sores bled open, the deep wounds stung,
but wetted tongues had torrents

of drowning words to sing.

Easy Street

I'm heading for Easy Street
two kids and a pack of valium
double lock door
sleep on the floor
and wait for it all to come back
– back the sound of your feet
the ugly things you said
the slam of the door, the slam
of your fist in my face, your feet
You said I did it on purpose
– bled.
You said I'd leave one way
– dead. Awake
I'm listening to every creak
sitting up cold in a sweat
hearing one sound repeat
On my feet
I check every window, each door
the floor under the beds
certain you must be here
waiting for me to sleep.
You said I wanted an easy life
couldn't take being a wife.
Heading back to the valium pack
this is living, for now
I'll wake up on Easy Street.

The List

This is her mother's pain
> for the other country you took her to
> for children sired but left unfed
> while you drowned life in hard drink
> for the other women you held
> while she nursed a tortured home
> through a lifetime of absences.

This is the child's fear
> for hands that tore up her night
> for the strangeness of your breath
> and the hardness of your lust
> for the differentness of your sex
> the stolen days and frightening streets
> and nightmare giants who wet her bed.

This is adolescent shame
> for a fourteen year old's trust
> crippled by a married man
> for the passion of seventeen
> dissipated through rape and then
> in state approved violation
> for that rape, for that death
> for the providence of hell on earth.

This is the woman's hurt
> for your questions, and your questions
> for your fist cracking in her face
> for the permanence of injuries
> the spirit crushed, the deeper scars
> for the baby in his grave
> children weeping in the storm
> sons beaten for being sons
> for the nights spent craving death.

This is her sense of loss
    for fathers who are not there
    for lovers who cannot love
    for brothers who daren't be
    for daughters flushed down the drain
    sons brutalised into men
    for love you took but couldn't give
    for the leaning you all did.

This is every door she can't open
    every street she can't walk
    every corner she can't stand on
    every word she cannot speak
    every tear you should have wept
    all the blood she cleaned up
    all the anger she hid away.

This is the chain she drags
    from the cradle to the grave.

This is my spell for you
    you fashioned this decoration
    you wear it, for a change.

The Trek

We had put our feet upon a tract of land
long since uncultivated.
The bones of ancient women crunched,
dry and brittle, under our feet.
Some of us were not equal to the trek
and fell to picking the bones,
squabbling for scrap with their sisters.
We left them to it.
The scream of vultures swirled the sky,
wanting us to drop. But the dreamed oasis,
a mirage of heat and hope,
kept us high-spirited and moving, ever on.
Now and then, with despair or some desire,
one would blaze herself upon the sky.
A roast that brought white-collared scavengers,
dark suits fluttering, to the feast,
their cawing to proclaim the heretic
a biological travesty.
We let them crow, this blinded breed,
and, sighting by a dream in red-eyed sun,
stepped foot by foot over bone dry desert,
thirsty for the dew to slake our feet;
dreamers of an oasis
where women and men could meet.

Words for My Daughter

Come, the cap of birth is dry,
my labouring is done, your cry
has split the world's roof.

Be comforted, the womb
returns to wrap around you.

Sweet darkness, velvet-blood
from which you came, as night
will cup you again, again

move you outward into light;
a brilliance to be danced in

is life. Your staggering steps
will grow to trust this earth;
it meets both sure and unsure feet.

That shifting pain will shape
the edges that define you.

Know the body that confines
is a new kind of freedom
to find the fullness of you.

Move through yourself. See,
the future is with child

and needs your labouring.
Be done with pasts, walk away.
I'll watch. I'll guard your back,

blinded by my own time. Go forward
from the shadows mothers cast.

As old women shrink, rich fruit
seeds into the garden.
I have been. Now you. So live,

we have both shed our tears
for miracles, for coming new.

In birth-sleep heavy at my breast,
love child, first comes the dream
and then the making true.

Borrowed from the Mother

It will not be a stranger
who washes you this last time.
I will unknot your clenched fist
from the gripped sheet, wondering
at the child still grasping life,
about your baby fist splashed
in a first bath, your mother's smile,
eyes masked with grief. She knew.
And knew when I took you, strong,
brown from wind and spray, took you
up hill to our unworn home.

I saw her eyes that day, wise,
wiser always than I was
who thought we'd outlast the love.
In the trailed song, spun dance,
the last lingerings, she stood,
set in the door frame, edged gold
as an old sun spilled into sea;
eyes hooded, black head dipped,
nodded, gave you over to me.

I learned you inch by month down
years that grew us both, the scar
by your mouth from a hook cast
when you taught me to fish, mark
of fire crimped on thigh, hot iron
of my temper. You cried out,
called me woman. Me, your wife.
But always your woman, holding
through long nights, parted days,
leaving space, crossing distance;
you drawing in on my reel.

You will not feel my hands now
though I have drawn fresh water
to wash you as child, and lover,
and husband, and friend. This bed
brought us, wedded to our end.
I'll cry no tears, beloved,
while death drives me to embrace
your mother's impassive mime.
But it will be no stranger
who washes you this last time.

Witchcraft

Make
nothing
except love
and love will make
you.

Gothic?

And if you open any door
you'll greet the bloodied visage
of gallant knight from days of yore.

But keep them closed, you'll sabotage
escape for damsels in distress
whose histories receive massage

to shape the unshapely truth.
That world of giant fantasy,
of goblin, demon, ghoul, is proof

that metaphor is the poet's key
to padlocked words. St George
did not set the princess free,

she was devoured. By him. The urge,
desire, that dragon lust, the roar
she'd been restrained against was hers.

Woman in Rags

above our tin shell ceiling
rain tacks down the roof
and the wind howls

miles high, mouth open
in a long looping wail
trailing skirts slap at our caravan

turning above us she is
a woman maddened
mourning in the dark for lost days

her wet rags slap again
sway us to some notion of grief
raged beyond consolation

desolation creeps into bed
we cease love making
pretend no desire to weep

she aches, inconsolable
but we know
her night will end in the sun

our separation will come

Storm Warning

You think she feels
gentled by you
– beware. Remember
the predator stares
loving stillness with a look.
The hidden claws unsheath
to hook deep in your heart.
If this woman starts
she might peel
that tough resistance
to reveal the need in you.
Oh, please expect
the marrow of your bones
to be sucked dry
and learn to cry now
for you will need
the healing salt of tears.
She will unleash
your fears and your desire.
She uses fire, her touch
will brand you, her kisses burn
all the long length of your skin.
Be careful man
if you come in to this woman
you may never sleep
soundly in your silent bed
again.

The Ashtray

She smokes brown cigarettes,
long and thin, the stubs
bent concertina dead ends
that she counts, keeping check
of the nicotine stain on her lungs.
Her evenings she spends
with a man, any man
who furnishes an alibi
while her craving drowns in whisky mac
and the made-up smile crumples
round a long thin smoke.
She laughs, flirts, invents
love as a nightcap
orgasm a ritualistic joke.
And the men? Well, she says
she has lost track of them by morning
when, bitter-mouthed, she reaches
to tip out the night's refuse;
a collection of brown, bent screws
in a stained glass dish.

Selling It

Sex sells motor cars
and chocolate bars, clothes,
pots and pans, those effervescent
ring-pull cans. With pouting lips
and curving hips, sex sells.
And macho man with instant
tan sells soaps and beer
and ropes a steer to demonstrate
a useful tool that will not rust.
My god, must we really have all this
and lust. But sex sells.
Sex sells pills and prams,
bottles sterilised and crams
high chairs, nappy pails, uses pins
and tins of powder, teething gells.
Sex swells
everybody's interest in themselves.
Ad-man's dream's a sex machine,
thick as yoghurt, smooth as cream,
smells like musk and is actually
a garden rake.
Take me, rake me. There's a slogan.
Sells well. But then sex will sell
anything from fish and chips
to holiday trips, jars of jam,
eggs and ham, never have enough.
Sex sells.
It's great stuff.

Squaring the Circle

The Howling

Full moon and the hot breath burns.
I am turning, and too late
for caution catch the last glimpse
of lost compassion. He waits,
does not see the claw unsheathed,
cannot guess I take my lovers neat.
He waits, wanting. I, wanting,
will not look into the glass,
could not outstare the fever.
Merciless, I will not hear
the howling as the beast consumes
his terrible innocence.

The Circle

Gently, he turns me – edges fold,
reflections in the mirror blur.
I hold distinction indistinct,
my instinct bitter to the last,
watching the sum of all my parts,
a patchwork stitched from this and that,
fray and scatter on the floor.
Nothing stands before me, is me,
nothing but what skin contains.
Tender, he touches – the outline splits,
self spills, extinguished, to abyss.

Death – death comes like this,
in loving arms, on a kiss.

The Fallen

Like the gods he thinks he wears
his incorruption as a skin, an aura
of light to be shed on a whim.
He would be branded with our sin,
marked by this earth he revels in.
Oh, he would know.
                        His words reveal
that innocence can't bleed from wounds
no matter how he bleeds, that sin
is by intent, that light cannot be shed.
It binds the bone, blueprints the flesh.
In this whore's bed, he still is him
– man undefiled. As the gods are, we are.
Innocent and knowing. Reconciled.

The Gathering

see me green dancing go
down the long meadow
swirl skirted in red
corn topped head
you sit high
your tractor ploughs sky
and I laugh teasing
mean nothing and everything

catching the spool you come
under the spell unwinding
we have begun my hands cup
I curve pull you in
you press earth holds us up
bond-cradled our divinity wins

we pull in harness strong
cider apples brown bread and the corn
filled we tramp skies into ground
seed for tomorrow make grey days
dance yellow gold fields
you furrow sure straight
I make mend wait
we unravel string bound us
we – ours – mine
time is thick rich soup spooned

obliquely I gaze at you
at the plains you span
certain now of endings
unsure how we began
earth under my feet shifts
and the hills toil turning
yellow for the boiling sun
brown to the reaper's blade
seasons turn the circle
the gathering is made

blighted with winter we sit
measuring out grain aching
from old bones warped hands
spring comes for the land
our season thread winding
has wound off the drum

While Pruning

Why now, while pruning, do you return
in the soft silk of a dying rose? The touch
of skin on skin has faded, not quite gone;
a ghost impression of the living thing.

So this rose, full-bud, half-opened lies
limp yet fragrant in my hand, dying.
Dying, sure, its petals never spread
waxing white bloomed in the sun. Perfumed,

as breath it taints the evening air, taunts
me with the might-have-beens. Tonight
nothing's clearer than this fresh green cut;
dead thorns draw blood. Could I have told

it was the love you kept that came between us,
the love you gave me that I couldn't hold.

Wild Cherry

An oriental woman visits our garden in the spring,
seeking pardon as she lays her white smooth cheek
against the rough and gnarled arm of age.
He has raged all winter against the emptiness
and now, incongruous, holds her tenderly to a muted sun.
Those black-hearted eyes, blacker in that palest cream,
have begun again this strange love affair,
this ill-matched dream, He bears her up,
she weighs him down, lightly, mightily.
She is his crown. Until dethroned
and stoned on grief, he mourns in weeds of green
while fissures deepen unseen in that dark shade.
Autumn, the renegade, strips him down to nakedness
and, shorn of dress, he stands, her legacy revealed,
his bent arthritic form scarred with blood-red seeds.

Bonfire

He sweeps the leaves
into a pile of autumn gold,
crisp brown, pale yellow,
burnished rust.
He does not speak
though we could almost touch
and if I talk
he will refuse to hear.
I do. He does.

So I keep picking apples.
Next door, he twists a paper torch,
touches flame
to what was green and spring
and now is dust.
He is husband to his wife
but I have none.
And worse, I earn my living
doing something strange
with words.

The rising smoke ghosts
other women from my past,
and has not changed.
I feel the heat, smell
my flesh begin to burn.

Praise the Lord

I remember sitting
on a flat bottom
stiff flat backed pew,
racked as a bracket
bent at right angles
to tighter attention,
rapt for the mention
of a little love
or a whole lot of compassion.

Praise the Lord!

Beside me, my need
spilled like a balloon
filled with black water
over edges, a big
blot of black hole
that wept and wobbled hugely,
pressed against strangers
Sunday best dressed.

Praise the Lord!

What size was yours?
A football – an airship
gargantuan – a mountainous host
– a Ghostbusters
junk-food swilling ghost
filling up and totally lost
on the man in the pulpit
who had all the answers
– religion. No question.

Praise the Lord!

I had those.

Praise the Lord!

Had them in my ears,
in my eyes, up my nose,
in my head, in my hands
in my soul, on my lap
in my coat, in my pocket
in my shoes, crawling
under my feet,
stuffed into my hat.

Praise the Lord!

So he beat on my brains
with his book full of answers
while chanting a homily
about the way cats died.

Praise the Lord!

Blind with the might
of eternal right,
no questions asked
he never realised,
though it killed the cat
curiosity survived.

Praise the Lord!

And thank god for that.

Ride with the Hunters

I have hidden from elephants
in this small Scottish village,
remembering to bolt the doors
of this thicket where I live.

I had forgotten that bricks crumple
like petals from a poppy flower
and wood splinters with as much resistance
as prairie grass under those leaden feet.

Try supplicating an elephant.
It's water off a mud bank to a raging bull
and in their quiet basking
merely makes them flap their ears.

So now I ride with the hunters
having cut my teeth on that same wood
and honed sharp talons upon mortar
while clawing my way out.

I have swooped down with the bats
and taken the eagles flight beyond their reach.
I learned from wolves
to slaver blood and spittle in the night.

And I can draw blood –
and I can bay at the moon.
And I don't fear elephants any longer,
only my own ferocity.

Critical Distance

Rattling over rooftops, she
hopscotches chimney pots, dots
around sounding her own shriek
(a parrot-like screech). She is
cock-a-hoop, looping the loop:
a sky-dive heroine lancing every long line
with razor sharp beak. She does
not slow down enough to speak,
nothing breaks her brass neck leap.

I'm standing in the gutter
muttering: see,
her shadow flutters up there
where jutting cornices
let rip her whoop-it-up
to a mad sky full of holes
that pecks of light shine through.

Too old and worn to make new,
I'm leaf laden, sodden
in the sewer stream, weighed down
with iron shoes rusted brown
and knowing that blood and bone
own my perishable, perilous way home
as she flies, crowing
to pick more holes in tattered skies.

The Caul

Parturition

Girl, I see your swollen shape,
eyes older than the broken hills.
I see your empty hand, the moon
curves to mimic where you stand.

Woman, you walk true to blood,
the last birth strain an acre
crossed in one leap, to fling you,
bind you, bring you from mystery
to grief. Why are you dancing?
Men would weep.

Issue

Coming into light, you cast
a yawling arc and trawl this place
for what is left of feeling.
Wonder aches our eyes. You stare,
this deep drifting fronts your pain.
Enraged, your anguish sucks in air.

Child, what is this you grow?
I knock my knuckles to the graze
on horny shell. What poison
swells your tongue, blanks your eye.
What blighted birthright this?
How do we recognise our dead –

don't laugh, don't love, don't cry?

Prematurely Beached

You might have walked here
but that tide was early.

You might have laughed
as they laugh, carelessly

turning card over card,
making jokes of each hand.

You might have turned the wind
round your dark head, found

the ripple of cloud building
darker banks in your eye.

And the head hard, splits free,
turns, exultantly free

suddenly from scissored flesh,
in the shivered wake of pain.

But you, wet knuckle unwound,
foot-birthed a short step.

You might have breached here
but death heard, hurried on.

Ceremony of Sorrow

You give me tea in a delicate cup
and only your hands are more brittle
than the pale china, wafer thin.
Today, we undertake an alien ceremony,
letting rules we don't know, mesh.
I feel the air strung out,
taut in need of vibration.
Our words escape like little birds;
a flutter, a dash for freedom.
We are two strokes; me the sharp, shiny hammer,
you the tense string. Poised,
I want to shatter your containment
in singing fine-bone splinters:
would have us both repaired
to coffee in thick brown mugs.

My spoon tinkles the unfamiliar cup,
death's fragile reckoning is not yet done.
It is too soon to mourn
and grief will guard its own gestation.
I take my tea, talk delicately.
Inside your shell, the demon stirs.

The Village

The village is potbellied,
though there are children
no-one here is young.
Parents are curtains,
cars and television sets;
hands holding coin they cannot spend,
eyes chipped to the splinter
of watching their patch.

The old guard the old;
they step slowly,
pressing down fence and pavement
as if fence and pavement both
have grown hard on the years.

The children snatch
at breath that eludes them,
harsh words and thin hands
claw the air.

Matthew

I wish, he says

making the word with his wet full mouth,
his eyes round beacons of delight
at all the words he can wish into life.
Small wide hands expand the sound
and draw the bigness of his wishes in the air.
He is all eagerness,
a colt quivering muscled shoulder at the taste of wind,
and belief's disciple
as hands of expectation clap in trust.
He just has to say and it is there.

A conjuror he is, no game.
This magic he makes is getting
tongue and teeth and lips
to name his dream.

The Last Bell

Seems like its always been
this chalk and mortar kingdom,
boundaries fixed, parameters set.
We've kicked against it
ineffectually,
and yet it was us too.
Enforced familiarity,
the shocking intimacy
of closed in spaces. Over years
our shell-shocked faces
grew less grim. We became
self-satisfied, tried and measured,
fitted in.

All we know is corridor
and the covers of a book.
How do we cook up life from that.
There could be fifty lean years
before the growing fat
on what we need to know.
But, tomorrow, we go.
They will ring the last bell,
we will pour
out those doors, running.
The last bell, steps flooding,
us – like lemmings.

Divisions

I am sieved through the mill; dust
in a wilderness laid bare
where the poor have no faces.
My sons look to me, their despair
feeding mouths that bite them.
The wheel turns. No assistance
beat their pens into ploughshares;
books pawned for chains. My resistance
the penance they pay.
I am finished. Hung bones, flesh thinned
by sheep fat on old grasses.
This southerly biting wind
strips down to rock – to the heart
scarred with words, rhythm, chords.
In my death song comes the art
from which my children draw swords.

Momentary Fox

Parting the pleated grass, he comes
soft-footed to the edge,
stops on the verge, without stopping;
a stillness in wind-rifted fur.
Not the usual slink of shape, he is
sharply defined, a self-assured fox.
Inside my car I, too, am stilled,
motionless with the moment
of wild outside the window.
His thoughts are not distracted,
they temper in his eyes,
wrought to incisive clarity.
He looks, without looking,
at our straight line world,
prints every brick and window
of sound and smell onto his brain,
notes the contradiction.
He stares at me but I am shadow,
my imprint missed. The lack of scent
disposing of me, casually.
Forged by certainty of self,
he has no morals; his rules
are down in black and white,
his world simpler than he knows.
He turns, without turning,
arrowed to earth, he goes.

Tidal Seal

Among rough rock she is a smooth slick,
a hump of black silk, sand-grained at the edges.
The living symmetry of her shape,
so unmechanical, stops me by her side:
stops me just a footfall short
of stepping on her ragged, wave-washed, life.
Her eye holds unreflected cloud, its own;
life sighs from her, the sound
of eye-lid closing, last beat loud;
the downstroke of a seagull wing silenced
by shush of wave on chattering shingle.

Her death cries out of her, a voice down wire
telegrammed through undistracted children
when warm wind shudders naked shoulder.
Folk in their caravans, unarrested,
drink the water of her dying. Coffee, tea,
syringed by kettle, cups into the vein.
And far inland the breath of her
sweeps a mountain, scoops a valley,
slithers through a city street.
The traffic trails its poisoned pap
round boxes full of fragile folk
packaged for the pound by pound of toil.

On my broken beach a young seal dies
but there, on pavements pitted by those feet
her death touches curdled cheeks,
tugs each sour strand of hair.
Prattling, they feed upon the fume of her
as wave on coming wave makes deaf-mute, all
dumbstruck by her small enormity.

Water of Lethe

I am
waiting for the dark
while night threads inshore
fingers round my calf
strokes my thigh.
Lovers, among other things,
were never this sure,
were mere diversion
as a breath held, drawn-in,
must be expelled.
I stand,
face the oncoming tide
while sand shifts
in the backwash of a breaker.
The sea sucks, sighs,
tugs, pulls, tries temptation
– a last love
whose benediction
burrows beneath my feet.
I sink,
cliffs crumble, stones fall.
I know this sea,
it wins all.

Absolutely

I've never been afraid of night
only of absolutes:
the complete, perfect, pure and
people who are absolutely right.

Though never having seen a star
at the distance of ten parsecs,
that magnitude can't be
so absolute as people are.

Despots say quite arbitrarily
and with unqualified conceit
that truth, at odds, is black and white.
Yet having lived contrarily

with only shades of grey to mark
the passage of both day and night,
I'm still afraid of nothing but
the absolute, absolute dark.

Excuses of a Romantic

Cleaning old canvas
with turpentine soaked wool
the splash of mud becomes green
sparking yellow.

I was young then
when primroses grew knee height,
new as lavender mornings
dusted with mist.

I was young then
when grass whispered my walk,
moss sighed when stepped on,
laughing, sprang back.

I was young then
when mouth held leaves in talk,
arms gathered trees, frogs conversed,
tongue tasted words.

Primroses in grass,
a trout tickled stream.
I was young then
and startled by birdsong.

Not Coming Home

How was I to know you would forget
and rearrange yourself in patterns unforseen.
the narrow bridge now yawns and houses ache
on empty ground that once spawned other schemes.

You hike yourself up torn hills that slept
under beech and ash. And where you have not reached
stride straight legged trees, a foreign breed.
A monumental move has put our memories

in the newly seamed breast pocket of old streets.
You've traded in a thousand births, and many deaths
have multiplied the number of unknown
faces that do not figure in my dreams.

Only the river winds its unworn course
and one stream is not enough to pin me back.
A penny paper token falls, floats off unseen.
How was I to know you would forget
and rearrange yourself in patterns unforeseen.

Homeless

skylight
       is bluebright gaps
 skydark   starsparked
spaces in black
        nightfaces
       the pale ghost
        of dawnmist
as the chillfist
       of daybreaks
        on bone
aches in her spine
    never rains but it pours
boardscreak
      into floorspeech
the windreeks
     a morning stench
of garbage
drenches
        her senses
and daygears up
       the street
in a crunch of trucks
       she wakes
outside everydoor
        inside
every mind a closedsign
finds gettingup
      is comingdown
and the ground
      is always hard

Three Ravens

One was a man, head filled
with fears attacking fears
hands filled with spears. A spore
has grown in the open cavity
between his lungs; its thirst
never ceased and from it no drop
of moisture was released.

One was a child, heart filled
with nightmare dreams,
head filled with schemes. He sat,
toothpicking at his flesh
while howls of outrage quarried
in the mess as round him grew
a wider, emptier space.

One was woman, she crouched
giving birth to blindness,
cradling her madness in deaf ears.
And yet the mountainous swell
of belly belied her growth
for at her heavy breasts
she sucked both.

Stock and Barrel

I am the keeper of a key
and sit in the night pool
nursing its silver threat.
Out in the street voluptuous voices
roll home in deep throats
and warm conspiracies:
intermittent shrieks
scar the soft pillows,
stalking each ribald remark.
I leach the night of sound,
borrowing; burying the words
in white paper, ever aware
of the hard key in my hand;
the power of the lock.
It is a metal sliver,
one turn to stock and barrel
when I am ready; one turn
and I am ready to
unlock the final door.

Old Horse

My soul is an old horse, is he?
Well, I'll take this rattle bag
of bones and shake him.
I'll make him cough.

Get ready to stretch your skin,
unknot arthritic knees.
Go on, paw the grass,
glare with your glassy eye,
you and me, we
got stuck with each other.
Sure, you could cry – see those trees,
bark, branch, leaf high.
See me, I could rush in there
and with bare hands braced
pillar to pillar, bring down that sky.
See the tide–hollowed cave,
it says come in here, sing.
Oh I could sing, I could shriek
so loud you would be proud
of the pain I'd make. Damn it to hell,
don't you think I'd give life itself
to be rid of the ache.
Really living, have you any idea
how much effort that takes.
Yes, I know there's sweet grass
and a meadow full of buttercup sleep
where old bones go to lie.
But you and me, brother, know we
don't want to live forever
but can't die. So get up,
draw your slack skin back in,
presume the shape you should be in,
lift your belly of the grass, pretend
if you must, that you're a stallion
but don't be an ass. I know
Death's a good friend but
I am telling you, let this pass.

Frog

The eyes have it
that infernal look
which predisposed a princess
now and then, to stoop.
It is the child stare
of intractable all–knowledge
a blank page contains.

Biting Through Skins

She peels the apple
the effort
of biting through skin
too much.
The peel, red-bitter, white-sweet
curls in snake coils
onto pale wood.
In the bowl
more apples gleam
blushing at their own kind
denuded.
Help yourself, she tells me
and I do
filling my hand with fruit.
The table snake browns
lazily
its skin shrinks.
A hiss
and my teeth cut
through bitter to the core.
Unwise I am always
biting through skins.

Poem with No Name

I am the new age man
footprints trekked across the changing sand
a line
shorter than the cobbles of my spine

I talk to deafened air
dropping stones in silent water where
a cave
might magnify the ripple into wave

I sing a hollow song
music from a pot stirred over–long
a flight
of mild fancy in a starving night

I carve on bitter stone
with torn nail and flesh stripped bone
a scribe
scratching unread law for his lost tribe

I build with howling fire
hot coals charring fingers that desire
a dream
of rivers flooded by a single stream

I fly through broken glass

bloodied wings torn fresh on every pass
a climb
that kills more love in me each time

I stop in lonely spaces
bedding down where barren rock displaces
a pain
echoing with need to know its name

I am the oldest thing on earth
fresh minted with unmeasured worth
a child
forever running naked in the wild

Biographical Note

Janet Paisley is a prize-winning poet, playwright, fiction, non-fiction, radio, television and screen writer who also writes poems, stories and radio drama for children. Awards include BAFTA and RTS nominations for the short film *Long Haul;* BBC, Sutton, Scotwrite and Canongate prizes, and the UK Peggy Ramsay award for her play, *Refuge*. In 1996 *Alien Crop* was shortlisted as Scottish Book of the Year and she was one of the first recipients of a Creative Scotland Award.

Previously a member of the Scottish National Theatre working party and SAC Scots Language Synergy, she is currently a member of the Cross Party Parliamentary Group for the Scots Language. She has held three Creative Writing Fellowships, received two Scottish Arts Council writers' bursaries, a playwright's bursary, edited New Writing Scotland, co-ordinated the first Scottish PEN Women Writers committee and initiated a Scottish cultural centre in Voronezh university, Russia.

A regular guest at national and international Festivals, her work has been translated into Hungarian, Polish, Italian, Catalan, Slovak, Lithuanian and Russian and performed at events as diverse as Glastonbury and Catalonia's *Cartographies of Desire*. Born in Ilford in 1948, she grew up in Avonbridge in central Scotland, six miles south of where she now lives in Glen Village near Falkirk. A mother of seven sons, single-parent, former teacher, pagan and practising witch who also gardens and sculpts in wood, she first published in 1979.

By the Same Author

Poetry:	*Reading the Bones, Ye Cannae Win* (monologues), *Biting Through Skins, Pegasus in Flight*
Fiction:	*Not for Glory; Wild Fire;*
Video:	*Images*
Film:	*Long Haul*
Plays:	*Refuge, Straitjackets, Winding String, Deep Rising, The Wild Bunch Abroad, Pair of Jacks*
Radio Plays,	*Diary of a Goth, Silver Bullet, Curds & Cream*
Other plays:	*Sooans Nicht, For Want of a Nail, Bill & Koo* (with Graham McKenzie).

The Wild Women Series

When women reach a certain age, they find themselves with half a lifetime's experience behind them: of life, men, maybe children, work – but they still retain their youthful energies. They have thrown off the restrictive influences of childhood, got bored with guilt. Any woman with spirit will want a change, something to challenge her mind and body; something to stir her emotions. Received wisdom will be no good: in her quest for real knowledge bland clichés will have no place. At last she can act, secure in her sexuality, her humanity, without conventional inhibitioins – at last she can be herself.

Beware anyone who crosses her or tries to tie her down or limit her. She is confident. She knows how to love, to be gentle, firm, kind and even cruel if she chooses. And yes, she can, if she wishes, be wild. If she is also a writer, her pen will be bright, sharp and unpredictable.

Light touch-paper and retire.

Titles in the Wild Women Series

Alien Crop – Janet Paisley
Wild Women of a Certain Age – Magi Gibson
Last Tango with Magritte – Lydia Robb
Good Girls Don't Cry – Margaret Fulton Cook
Telling Gestures – Joy Pitman

Forthcoming:
Selected Poems of Sheena Blackhall
The Wild Women Anthology
and . . .